WORCESTER
IN OLD PHOTOGRAPHS

WORCESTER
IN OLD PHOTOGRAPHS

WILLIAM & MICHAEL DOWTY

ALAN SUTTON
1986

Alan Sutton Publishing Limited
Brunswick Road · Gloucester

First published 1986

British Library Cataloguing in Publication Data

Worcester in old photographs.
1. Worcester (Hereford and Worcester)—History
I. Dowty, Michael
942.4′48082   DA690.W9

ISBN 0-86299-295-8

Typesetting and origination by
Alan Sutton Publishing Limited.
Printed in Great Britain
by Redwood Burn Limited.

INTRODUCTION

When I was asked to compile a book of photographs on Worcester, there seemed no better way for me to pay a belated tribute to my father, William Ward Dowty 1887–1979, than through his photographs of the city in the 1920s and '30s. By chance, publication coincides with the family photographic centenary, giving me what I hope is an acceptable reason to preface it with some potted Dowty history.

It was in 1886 that my grandparents, William & Laura Dowty, left their native Evesham and moved to the Abbey Pharmacy, High Street, Pershore, where grandfather took over the practice of a Mr Drew who had at one time been apothecary to the exiled Napoleon on St Helena. Grandfather expanded the practice to include photography and it was presumably he who added 'Rembrandt House' to the address, thereby advertising his ability and willingness to not only treat bodily afflictions with medicaments, but also paint facial features with light.

Having arrived in Pershore with two children, my grandparents produced a further six during the next fifteen years, the complete family being, in order of appearance: John, Jessie Maria, Joseph Masters ('Masters' was grandmother's maiden name), William Ward, Robert, Arthur Golding and, finally, the twins, Edward Flexton and George Herbert. Grandmother's pride in her sons was family legend, a part of which records that when an irate daughter-in-law once accused her: 'If George were to rob a bank, you would find nothing wrong with it!' she was silenced by the crushing response: 'If George were to rob a bank, he would have a perfectly good reason for doing so'.

Backed (or driven) by this maternal force, my father and his six brothers grew up to have successful and – I hasten to add – honest businesses; one in farming, two in industry, one in pharmacy and three in photography. They helped each other out in difficult times, and their sister devoted much of her life to their interests, once she had recovered from the double tragedy of becoming a World War I widow and losing her only child. Her husband, Sidney Fell, was articled to a Worcester solicitor when the war intervened and cost him his life. It was through

5

information received from him that my father came to buy the once-renowned but by then sadly run-down business of T. Bennett & Sons at 8, Broad Street.

Tom Bennett had established his business in 1856 (the year, incidentally, in which my grandfather was born) and it had flourished under his guidance to the extent of enjoying Royal patronage on several occasions. His sons, however, were of lesser calibre and apparently tippled the business down the drain, once Tom was no longer on earth to curb their tendencies. Eventually, one died in circumstances that were never satisfactorily explained, whilst the other took an extreme measure of potassium cyanide, a year later, in the first floor room over the shop.

The unhappy ending of the Bennett era had an ironic echo, for on the 25 February 1913 when my father was in Worcester to complete the purchase of the business, grandfather died suddenly at Rembrandt House, which was a great shock and a sad loss to family and community alike. For my father, it marked the beginning of what was perhaps the bleakest period of his life as he attended to matters at home and struggled to revive a newly-acquired, near-extinct responsibility that earned him no more than 7s 6d during his first three weeks of ownership.

His survival and ultimate success owed something to the effort put into the early Pershore years, when much time was spent cycling around the district, weighed down by a bulky halfplate reflex camera, producing local postcard views for sale in village shops and post offices, or searching for newsworthy events, photographs of which regularly found their way into Berrow's *Worcester Journal*'s weekly pictorial supplements, giving his name frequent publicity over a wider area.

Virtually all of his photographs in this book were taken on Thornton Pickard or Sanderson halfplate cameras. When I joined the family business in the late 1940s, my own professional baptism was on the very same cameras and I can testify that they were not best suited to some of the livelier subject matter undertaken. They were, nevertheless, lovely instruments and ideal for teaching the novice not to become 'trigger-happy', for even in those days negative-material was expensive enough. In more experienced hands they produced memorable results, and many of my father's negatives are so good and full of interest that I have made a point of 'lifting' sections of some of them, to better reveal the pictures within the picture.

I grew up at 8, Broad Street in the '30s and '40s, at a time when there was no great shame in 'living on the premises'. Several of our business neighbours did likewise, finding that it made sound economical and practical sense. Our own domestic and working accommodation were both excellent and spacious, with splendid panoramic views of the city from the fourth floor (better still for those brave enough to climb on the roof). From the lower windows we were able to study everyday city life and watch the carnivals, military parades and other passing events, including the hill-climb competitors heading for Shelsley Walsh. Internally a steady flow of pedestrian traffic made its way to and from the studio: portrait sitters, pedigree pet owners, the inventor with his latest brainchild, ballroom dancers and their trophies, and wedding parties laying confetti trails as liberal as the scatterings of 'hares' in a paper-chase. The variety was endless.

For me, my father's photographs are the perfect evocation of an amiable age, when the commissionaire sprayed scent up and down the aisles of the Silver

Cinema during intervals, and you could tell (even blindfold) that you were in Woolworth's, by the slipperiness of the waxy-wooden floor and the unique smell representing a blend of all that was on offer at 'nothing over 6d' – or less. And then there were the simple pleasures of penny bus rides, or watching those small-change containers wiring their overhead way from cashier's cubicle to counter in the larger shops and stores. Debatably higher on the pleasure-scale were visits to the Theatre Royal, whose orchestra's inglorious strains rivalled those of many a café trio for awfulness as they shredded the overture or heralded the on-stage imminence of a lesser breed of Tiller Girl, referred to in the programme as '6 Dancing Lovelies 6' – the number repeated in case you got it wrong the first time. But the debit side of memory haunts me with seasonal odours from the nearby hop warehouse that put me off beer for life.

To supplement my father's work, I have included a selection of contemporaneous advertisements, mostly from publications that he helped to illustrate – the Official Guide to the City of Worcester and various Worcester Operatic Society programmes. Apart from the entertainment value, they are intended to serve as reminders of city trading names no longer in evidence. Finally, a few of my own photographs have been 'slipped-in', partly to demonstrate that nostalgia is not the sole right of any one age or age group, but mainly to record an unfading gratitude to my parents for their constant help and encouragement up until the year in which they both died. Without that help I might not have followed in the family photographic footsteps and this book would not have appeared.

Michael Dowty.
March 1986

W.W. Dowty in his Pershore days, with the halfplate reflex plate camera.

W.W. Dowty as he will be best remembered in this Broad Street portrait. Having served with the R.A. in France during the later stages of World War I, he was rarely seen without his 'Gunners' tie and British Legion badge. Like most of his professional contemporaries, W.W.D. was primarily a portrait and wedding photographer, so that the following examples of his work represent the lesser-known side of his photographic nature. He took his photography very seriously, but liked to spread a little laughter as he did so – I have done my best to compile a book of which he would have approved.

Girls Friendly Society members display their millinery-crowned heads at a Worcester Diocesan Festival in June 1922. There will be an abundance of hats throughout the book.

The best known, most photographed view of Worcester, seen here as it appeared in the 1920s. To the extreme left is Dent Allcroft's glove factory, whilst to the right, fronting on to the towpath is Courtenay's Worcestershire Sauce works, although any self-respecting, 'faithful' citizen knows that there has only ever been one 'Original and Genuine' sauce of that name.

The same features, as seen from the Hylton Road side of the bridge and at a later date. By now, Dent's presence is advertised in white letters on the factory chimney. The bridge was originally opened in 1781 and had a width of 24 feet. It underwent a change of appearance in 1847, when it was widened by 8 feet by the addition of cast-iron arches and parapets – a modification not generally thought to have enhanced its appearance.

Looking east across the bridge to Bridge Street. The combination of brick carriageway and tramlines must have made bridge-crossing hazardous in wet weather. The sauce manufacturers, Mellor & Co., were established in the early 1870s, according to available information, but were missing from here not long after this photograph was taken (see page 16).

The bridge, from the North Parade side, showing what is, presumably, preliminary work for further widening and modification. Behind the interested group of spectators to the left, a tram is heading for St John's, dating the photograph at not later than 1928.

A closer look at the workmen – who are now not working, but looking at the camera.

By 1931, when this was taken, bridge widening was completed, though there was still work to be done on its approaches.

This detail from the above photograph shows 'Mellor's Wall' converted to dual-purpose use in appealing for funds for General Infirmary extensions and advertising a 'Worcester Shopping Week'.

A further detail from the facing page. Properties in South Parade and the tower of All Saints Church.

The reconstructed bridge, looking west to Cripplegate Park. On the extreme right are temporary seating and other constructions being erected for the visit of Edward, Prince of Wales, who opened the bridge, the park extension, and also the Infirmary extensions on 28 October 1932.

River trips have long been an attraction for residents and visitors alike. Here, the steamer *Holt Castle* has just left its South Quay landing stage and is making its heavily-laden way upstream to Holt Fleet, passing a line of parked charabancs on North Quay.

Water for enjoyment is one thing; floods are an entirely different proposition, no matter how visually attractive they might be. Many Worcester people have known the annual misery of having their homes flooded, quite apart from the possibility of being marooned in them or unable to reach them. Here are two delightful demonstrations of the horse's value in solving the latter problem. None of the passengers in these Hylton Road views got their feet wet – but W.W.D. must have done.

Detail from page 19.

Supplies for the stranded, delivered to a first floor window in a champagne crate.

Take away the back-up team and the watery associations and this diver might pass for an astronaut. He is about to plumb the depths of the Salwarpe at Hawford, to the north of the city.

Continuing the watery theme: the Lifeboat Day Carnival of August 1924, photographed from a first floor window at 8, Broad Street. The lady on the left is selling Lifeboat flags.

Entry No.7 provided by T.S. Townsend & Sons Ltd, Albion Flour Mills. It is difficult to say what the float represents; it appears to be a mobile fortune-teller's tent with nurses in attendance, possibly to revive clients affected by over-robust predictions.

Britannia passes (in greater detail on next page). The shops in the background are: L.R. Glenn's (Men's Outfitters); R.S. Skan (Tobacconist); George & Welch (Chemist – it was here, at 68, Broad Street, that Mr Lee and Mr Perrins gave birth to their 'Original and Genuine' Worcestershire Sauce); Edgar Chapman (Tailor).

Miss Mabel Sneed's dancing pupils are as engulfed in flowers as is their transport.

Detail from page 24.

A rare example of the GWR running (nearly) on tramlines.

Workers at Chidley's – and a little girl – taking time off to watch the procession and resourcefully adapting the materials of their trade to the comfort of their elbows.

Youthful enthusiasts following the procession down Broad Street.

Rather more sedate are these two views of a 'Battle of Worcester' pageant, staged at the County Ground in July 1920 in aid of Worcestershire County Cricket Club. It looks a highly ambitious, costly production.

From the outdoor theatre of carnival and pageant to the real thing: the Theatre Royal in Angel Street, which was the third theatre to occupy the site since 1779, having itself been built in 1877. In this view, passers-by mask much of the poster for *My Old Dutch*, the only other readable information being that it was 'A Play in Four Acts'.

These out of focus children placed themselves on the edge of the negative as W.W.D. photographed a carload of (according to the poster) 'Famous Denville Players' to publicize 'An Important Engagement For A Season Of Popular Plays', commencing on 8 June with *The Story Of The Rosary*. Sounds thrilling.

It is, perhaps, more of a car overload and it is doubtful whether any amount of cranking will get the company moving.

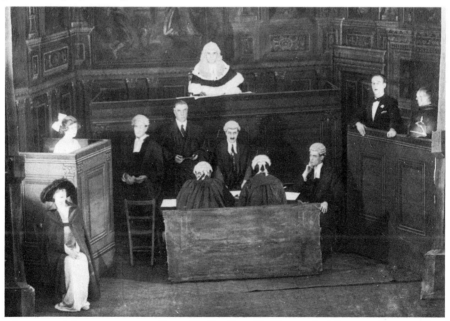

This may not have any connection with the Denville Players, but it was a Theatre Royal production. It has been suggested that it might have been *Trial By Jury*, since some of the protagonists seem to be pleading their case in song.

MONDAY, MAY 3rd

1.   OVERTURE
Ernest Arnold and Theatre Orchestra

2.   RED FRED
The Wonder on the Wheel.

3.   VIOLET GAYNOR
A Charming Singer.

4.   ASTOR & ASTORIA
Novelty Jugglers.

5.   CLAYTON & JACKIE
Fiddle and Feet.

6.   INTERVAL
Ernest Arnold and Theatre Orchestra.

The Theatre Royal programme for Monday, 3 May 1937, with Billy Russell at No. 10 in a stunningly varied menu.

35

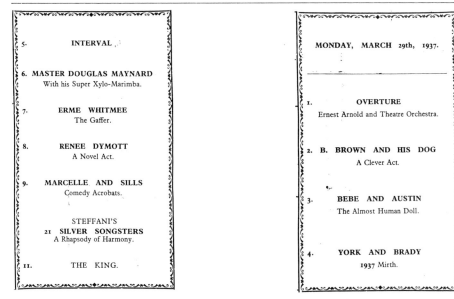

The Variety Bill for Monday, 29 March 1937. The adverts were exactly the same as those on the previous pages.

Safety curtain. Many Worcester theatre-goers will recall the curtain hurtling down at the interval, thereby fulfilling safety regulations and providing them with some reading matter.

Final curtain. The last audience leaving the Theatre Royal on 28 May 1955. Quoting from the poster: 'Frank H. Fortescue's Famous Players. Our Last Week. For Adults Only – The Daring Play: *FORBIDDEN FRUIT*. Friday Night Only: *SHOULD A WIFE TELL?* This Play Is For Adults Only'. No wonder it had to close. (Michael Dowty)

And now, for the next few pages, the 'celluloid theatre'. Here, we see the shooting of a scene from *The Tavern Knight*, made in the early '20s. Why W.W.D. was photographing it has never been clear to me, but I am glad that he did, for it gives me a chance to relate a favourite story told to me many years ago, concerning a man seeking work as an 'extra'. Having confirmed to a Casting Director that he could ride a horse, he was sent off to be kitted-out as a Roundhead before reporting back to Edgar Street. The following narrative is as I recall it – unexpurgated: 'So I gets back to Edgar Street and there doesn't seem to be anything going on, so I decides to have a ride down Severn Street – and bugger me, who should be riding up the other way but King Charles hisself! And he says: "Good morning" and I says "Good morning, Sir" and he says: "I don't know about you, but I was just going in to the pub to 'ave one. Would you care to join me?" So, "Thank you very much, Sir," I says, and we tethers our horses and goes inside and up to the bar. "Now then", says King Charles, "what you going to have?" "Well, Sir", I says, "if it's all the same to you, I'll have a double scotch". "You'll have a pint and bloody-well like it!" he says.'

When Fritz Lang's 1926 epic, *Metropolis*, came to the Scala Cinema, the book of the film was available from Marks & Spencer, inspiring some extravagantly-worded window publicity.

There is no way of knowing if this Scala audience was there for *Metropolis* or some other sensation. What is certain is that they were sitting in Worcester's best-loved and most atmospheric cinema.

The Silver Cinema, Foregate Street, standing next door but one to Foregate Street railway bridge, the western end of which is to the left. The Odeon Cinema has occupied the site – and those of its right-hand neighbours – since 1950.

The Arcade Cinema was at Nos 4 and 5, St Swithun's Street, sandwiched between Lettice the draper and Noake Bros, the shoe shop. No reference can be found concerning Charles Rock, Weybury, or his morals, so they must be presumed to have been not very nice.

The interior of the Arcade, making it look tiny and intimate from this position . . .

... but entirely different when viewed from the screen. At a rough estimate, the auditorium would have seated around 500.

A typical publicity stunt, setting-off from outside the cinema.

The prints on this and the facing page are from one negative which has suffered the ravages of time. The event was another example of the cinema and motor industry publicizing each other. No reference can be found to any film titled 'A First Auto', so the connection has to remain a mystery. The cinema was the Scala.

Still outside the Scala, featuring a mini-fleet of taxis in Angel Place. Behind them is the Duke of York public house, and to its right, Electra House, the home of Abell & Smith's Electrical Co. Ltd.

A closer, head-on view of two of the cars shows that one of them is left-hand drive. All three were from the same stable, as identified from lettering above their radiator grilles: 'Crown Hotel Garage, Broad Street, Worcester'.

And still outside the Scala, for an altogether bigger event, featuring a good cross-section of society and a dog, who is not unlike the one that gained his immortality in the service of His Master's Voice.

This section is merely aimed at drawing attention to the large bottle in the pocket of the boy at the centre – it might well be one of those lovely flip-up tops that used to be on Corona bottles. Corona Ginger Beer was one of W.W.D.'s favourite drinks, with a crate of four bottles costing 1/3d delivered to the door and 3d back on the crate.

A smaller 'All Boys Together' outing on the point of departure from the North Quay. The Electricity Works is directly opposite.

A 'girls' equivalent is almost ready to leave from Hylton Road (close to the Electricity Works).

Enter, the private motorist. What a lovely age it was, when, as a change from visiting the photographer's studio, the photographer would come to you and photograph the latest pride and joy with the family posing in it. Wouldn't happen too often nowadays.

This, I understand, was a privately owned taxi. It was certainly immaculately turned-out, with its high polish extended to the can of Shell Motor Spirit on the running-board. Even the spare wheel is wrapped, to keep the dirt out. The filler-cap mascot is a suitably streamlined version of Felix the Cat, tail straight out behind him.

This could quite easily be a chauffeur-driven dog. Something about his expression suggests that he might even be titled. It's not always possible to tell from just looking at a photograph.

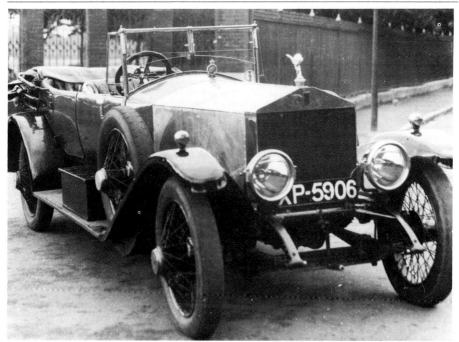

The height of opulence: a Rolls imperiously stands at the gates of Pitchcroft.

The depths of repair: an Austin pathetically cringes in the sick-bay at Thorne's Garage in The Butts.

Steam moving the 'moving spirit'. The traction-engine was hauling a hefty load of two massive tanks. The location isn't easy to pinpoint, but it could have been the GWR siding in Pitchcroft, looking across the river towards the Hylton Road tannery.

'Renowned of Petrols' is what the letters stand for at this undernourished-looking filling station. It may be hard to believe, but I have an idea that this was the beginnings of what is today a much fatter establishment at Cherry Orchard, Bath Road.

Stationary staff at Shrub Hill. A trio of Inspectors at the foot of the footbridge steps.

W.W.D. took very few railway photographs. This one, split into two sections, was on the occasion of an outing for employees of Kay's and shows them waiting on the east-bound platform at Foregate Street station. The date would be somewhere around the mid-twenties.

Down to three wheels with this daring combination. I have no idea what breed of machine it is, but it was probably no more unnecessarily noisy than today's models.

Peaceful pedal-power at last. A pageant of the bicycle which was put on (I believe) by St John's Cycling Club.

A small gathering of cyclists in the Trinity. These two prints and the one on the facing page are again sections from one negative.

The boy who can't afford a bike – not even at the prices overleaf. He is obviously desperately poor, his boots falling apart, their soles breaking away from what is left of the uppers. He sucks a heavily and dirtily-bandaged finger and stands in sharp contrast to the confidently smiling girls behind him. This is the debit side of life in the '20s.

Curry's were our neighbours at Broad Street and very handy for all sorts of things besides bicycles and their associated bits and pieces. In this display, however, the emphasis is heavily on cycling matters and costs in 1925. A fairy-cycle in front of the left-hand window was 39/6, whilst full-size machines were from £3 10s 0d and the most expensive, visible model had an £8 8s 0d ticket on it. Spare tyres ranged from 2/11 to one at a reduced price of 8/11, and a spare wheel without tyre would set you back 5/11.

Next to low prices there's nothing like a spot of sunlight for brightening a day, or – according to the International Stores – the wash.

"*Ethel!*

Mr. Lasthope is
coming to supper
this evening. Be
sure and order a
pork pie from
Hopkins!"

Yes, Madam.

You always insist that we
have them from there.

W. H. HOPKINS

*People get like
that over Hopkins'
Pies. Their Butter
is equally popular
too.*

28, BROAD STREET, WORCESTER.   **'Phone 865.**

Let us now have a break of several pages for some uninterrupted commercials.

A second mention for Webb's brings us to the city centre where tramcar No. 9 is heading for Bath Road. The electric tramway in Worcester had a comparatively short lifespan of around 22 years.

This is a bit of a puzzle – tramcar No. 9 has moved but a few yards since the last page, yet in that short time it has had a change of passengers and lost its driver into the bargain. The van passing on its nearside belongs to Lawley's, the china shop, which was situated just out of the photograph on the right.

A portion of the above view, putting more emphasis on the Foregate in the distance. A street banner publicizes a visit by the 'Band of H.M. Gordon Highlanders – with Pipers and Dancers'. The pedestrians crossing the street have a 'Lowryesque' quality.

Looking towards the Cross from High Street, with Cassidy's clock standing at 3.22 p.m.

Worcester Cross in early morning sunshine, seen from the corner of St Nicholas Street.

The Foregate, from the Cross. On the right is Lennards' shoe shop on the corner of St Nicholas Street. Behind it stands the Hop Market Hotel.

Foregate Street, photographed from near the Public Library and looking towards the city centre.

Two impressions of Broad Street from its lower end, as it was during the tram era and then in the early 1930s when the tracks had been removed. In the later view, the large, distant chimney marks the position of No. 8, sandwiched between the Midland Bank and Curry's. Today, all three properties have been rebuilt as a bigger bank.

Angel Place in the '20s, with its bus shelters, a corner of the Scala and the Sheep Market, better remembered, perhaps, for the Saturday market stalls that featured for many years. Children of the '30s will have fond memories of being able to 'trade-in' or swap their comics there.

The activity in the background fascinated me in the above view. Hence the inclusion of this section, showing a peculiar breed of omnibus in which the driver apparently had his own private 'cocoon', insulating and isolating him from his passengers. The registration number was CA 7090 and the front panel advertising was for ILO Lubricating Oils and Greases.

Worcester Cross without a tram in sight. This might have been somewhere near the end of the era, although the two foreground Midland Motor Services buses are more likely to have been operating on country rather than city routes. An enlargement of this photograph has featured in the Bradford & Bingley Building Society offices since they first opened in Foregate Street and may be seen at their new premises on the Cross.

Midland Red bus shelter and (behind) Travel Bureau on the Cross, next to St Nicholas Church.

High Street before widening. On the right, W. & F. Webb's and its further neighbours, The White Tea Rooms and Mann's the ironmongers, stand out of line, creating quite a bottle-neck. The photograph was taken from near the Guildhall and obliquely locates two more well-known Worcester names: Spark & Co. the Music Shop, and George's Restaurant. Both premises are now the M.E.B. Showrooms.

A crowded pavement in front of J.W. Cassidy's the jewellers, 64, High Street. The family business is now continued by David Cassidy, but from a new address at Crown Passage, Broad Street, surely the most visually pleasing of Worcester's recent developments.

Two more busy pavement scenes from the opposite side of the street. Once more, these are sections from one photograph and it should be just about possible to see how they link up.

Apart from one fleeting appearance at the end of the Carnival (page 29) and a back view in lower Broad Street (page 75), the police have been noticeably absent from the proceedings. Spreading their good-natured presence over two pages ought to help redress the balance. They are engaged in a little light-hearted crowd control. Ah, Happy Days!

Nothing to do and all day to do it in. I forget who said that, but it seems appropriate to this tranquil, late afternoon scene in Broad Street.

Plenty to do and hardly time to think. It's easy to forget the time when policemen were our only traffic lights. This one's arms are busily semaphoring at the top of Broad Street.

Loitering with intent – intent to sell Berrow's *Worcester Journal*, then advertised as being 'The Oldest Newspaper in Great Britain', but long-since promoted to the status of 'Oldest Newspaper in the World' (someone must have dropped out of the field). Berrow's celebrates its 300th anniversary in 1990. In the window behind this relaxed row of newsvending humanity is an opened copy of the 'Pictorial Supplement', probably with at least one of W.W.D.'s photographs in it.

The photographs on these two pages are of subject matter coming under the loose heading of 'Street Trading'. It's all a question of whether you are pushing yourself, an ideal, a product, or a load of something on a cart. In this view, a coachload of — to me — unsavoury-looking individuals is drawn up in Sansome Walk, behind the Shirehall, anxious that one of their number should get the Lygon's share of the vote.

The 'Imps' were apparently a form of Young Conservatives, their full title being 'Junior Imperialist League'. I wonder if any of them forsaw the future in which a surfeit of imperialism would turn us all metric.

Selling fruit from barrows in the Trinity, at the corner of Mealcheapen Street.

Just around the corner in Mealcheapen Street, rarely as free of people as it is here. The 'something' on the cart is a load of planks.

The following selection of frontages, windows and wares begins with the truly astounding 'Double-Sided Celebrity Records', featured in Spark & Co's window, with names like Melba, Cortot, Heifetz and Caruso on the HMV label.

David Greig's were making a big thing of tea and Danish bacon. The teas were backed by the slogan 'A Luxury You Can Afford', aided by a warm smile from the young lady on the opposite page.

L.H. Fearis (corner of Foregate Street and Shaw Street) went in for precision presentation of their meat. You could hardly ask for a neater frontage than this.

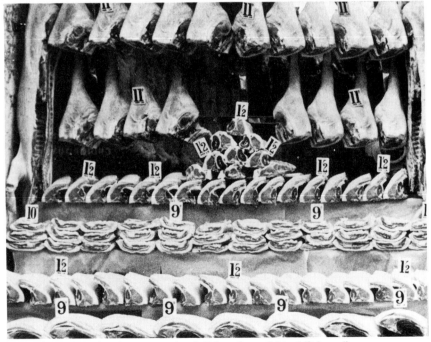

The left-hand window in greater detail. Prices from 8*d* to 1/2*d* per lb.

The right-hand window and some even lower prices. Here, the range is from only 4*d* with nothing over 1/3*d* per lb.

Another department of L.H. Fearis, offering 'Today's Special Line'.

A more robust approach to trading in flesh at an unknown butcher's in the Shambles.

Something on which to cook your meat or whatever – and 'Meals can be cooked without attention' proclaims Jackson's poster. Not only that, but all but one of the models displayed have Chippendale-influenced legs.

Fruit for afters, from A.F. Eden, who was at the time telling all and sundry about his newly-installed 'National' cash registers.

Pickfords – offering to save you the frustration of railway station queues by selling GWR and LMS tickets at no extra charge.

The British Shoe Coy Ltd had its windows packed with bargains from around 10/6d up to 25/0d. And if you decided to wear your new pair there and then, you would be able to see them reflected in a gleaming, brass footplate as you closed the shop door behind you.

When the trams were still running past their High Street door, Boots were not only Cash Chemists but also Cash Stationers, besides having an upstairs window filled with trunks and suitcases.

Woolworth's — and wasn't it fun when they had proper windows? This one being devoted to toys has an invitation in the top left corner: 'Our Toy Department is well worth a visit. Don't forget to bring the kiddies to see the Funny Old Chucker & Father Christmas. They will be delighted'. Wonder who 'Funny Old Chucker' was.

What a choice there was at 6d a time — picture cubes, doll's tea sets, furniture and kitchen utensils, building bricks, cricket balls with a real shine on them, tennis balls, too, and those solid rubber ones that bounced so well and were indestructible — unless the puppy got hold of them. All these toys, plus the books, were in this window at that one price.

A Gillette window at R.S. Skan & Sons, 69, Broad Street.

85, High Street.

58, Broad Street, and a comprehensive range of Battersby hats, plus the 'guarantee of an exact fit in any type or style'.

The selection of windows and frontages ends with three 1937 Coronation displays. With this first one, the name of the shop isn't known, but there is no escaping the name of the favoured manufacturer. Bang in the middle of the window is the 'Amazing New All-Wave Superhet – only 10 Guineas'.

Spiller's Stores modestly kept their name out of the window, thus allowing Bird's to take full advantage of the Coronation coinciding with their own centenary.

Fearis's effort on Bird's behalf was considerably more striking and professional – the product really does appear to be crowned with success.

The outward manifestation of a different success story. A pricey piece of automobiliousness parked outside Barclay's Bank in the Foregate, whilst its owner deposits his next million – or could he be drawing a bit out to pay the chauffeur who so patiently leans against the radiator grille?

The home (or former home) of someone in a lower income bracket. An old house in Lowesmoor.

Also in Lowesmoor, the Boat Inn, reintroducing the earlier liquid theme, in refreshment form.

These gentlemen take more water with it. W.W.D. would have enjoyed photographing
Cadbury's Fire Brigade, having himself been a member of the Pershore Brigade, whose
appliance was never known to be as heavily manned as this one which always puts me in
mind of the Keystone Cops.

In this view, a clinically wholesome workforce is engaged in the production of what seem to be small cakes at Cadbury's Blackpole factory.

Now, here's quite a good puzzle picture, having possible links with the last subject. The question is this: Are these people watching an outdoor cake-decorating competition, and is that a discarded icing-bag on the ground? . . .

No, on both counts. As you now see, what is actually taking place is a devastatingly decorous demonstration of conflagration control. (A lady is showing how to put out a fire.)

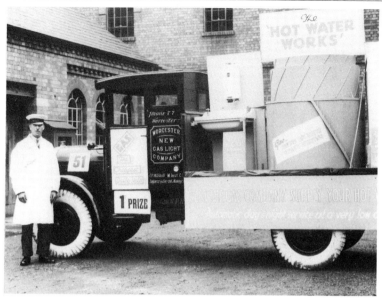

The pallidly-lettered slogans on this winning carnival float convey the message: 'Let The Gas Company Supply Your Hot Water – Automatic day and night service at very low cost'. As a supporter of 'Gas Power', I applaud, though can't help remembering an unfortunate piece of journalism in the *Worcester Evening News*, some years ago: 'It's Quicker by Gas!' said the advertisement, next to the news item recording a man's suicide by putting his head in a gas oven.

THE MODERNS
ADHERENTS TO MR. THERM

Gas- WINTER'S NATURAL SUBSTITUTE
FOR THE MODERN SUN - WORSHIPPER

WORCESTER NEW GAS LIGHT CO.

This man also had his head down as he performed an altogether happier feat of escapology from the sack-hoist at the Angel Street Hop Warehouse in May, 1922. If his views on hops matched mine, he would have had every incentive to make a quick getaway.

Which he did. Here, he has escaped from the strait-jacket and is on the point of being eased-down by helping hands.

The escapologist disappeared into the crowd, leaving behind the array of posters on the Corn Exchange wall – Lord John Sanger's Circus with a boxing elephant named 'Carpentier'; free demonstrations of 'Eezall' at the Public Hall; 'Why Germany Was Hated'; Worcestershire at home to Lancashire; the partially hidden name of G.A. Studdert-Kennedy, due to speak at the Annual Meeting of Worcester Christian Social Service Union.

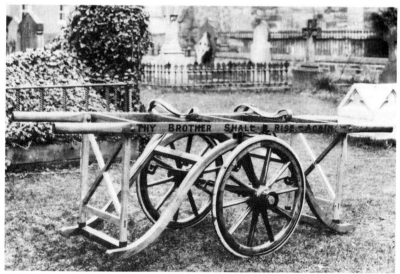

Although there may ultimately be no escape for any of us, here, at least, is some good news for brothers (and sisters) from J.L. Larkworthy & Co, manufacturers of this hopefully-worded vehicle: 'Thy Brother Shall Rise Again' is the message.

This kitten has been forced into a packet several sizes too small for it. I hope it wasn't W.W.D.'s own idea, because if there is one thing that proper cats and kittens loathe, it is being pushed into silly situations. We all now know the meaning of 'forced feeding'. As to the product itself, my own knowledge is limited to a little rhyme told to me by an old (and sadly late) friend: 'High over the fence leaps Sunny Jim, For "Force" is the food that raiseth him.'

On the other hand, this lady has outgrown her costume – unless the mini-skirt was an earlier creation than hitherto supposed.

The young woman pictured here, so shamelessly flaunting her bottles, deserved to be incarcerated in the establishment opposite, for her part in publicizing yet another 'Worcestershire'. If it is true that imitation is the sincerest form of flattery, then Lea & Perrins ought to hold the record for having been flattered more times, in more countries, than any other known Company.

The County Gaol in Castle Street, which was built in 1813 and in use for over a century. It is likely that W.W.D. photographed it around the time of its closure in 1922.

The gaol had other uses and formed an agreeable background for commercial photographs of cars. Today, no one in their right mind would entertain the idea of posing the latest model in the middle of the road at the lower end of Castle Street.

Some commercial vehicles. Much the same thing applies as did to the private car – people loved to have them photographed. Nowadays, they simply use them, or try to keep out of their way. In any case, they're hardly as photogenic as their ancestors. Jack Thompson, the fishmonger, must have been pretty pleased with his new lorry.

Skan, Taylor's van was actually one of three that were lined up in front of their Shaw Street premises.

You may be as surprised as I was to learn that Worcestershire Farmers Ltd were as old as this photograph proves. It was taken in June, 1929 when a consignment of bananas was being unloaded at North Quay.

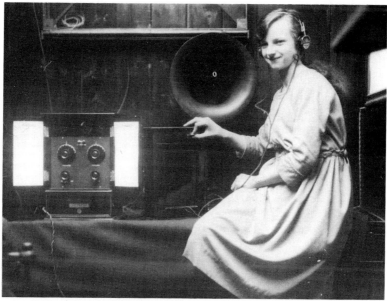

And now to what might be described as 'Commercial Radio'. In the photograph, Miss Katie Coomber is seen with one of the first GEC sets at her father's Tything premises in about 1928. I recently went to see her brother, Mr Robert Coomber, at the company's new address in Croft Walk, and he told me that his sister was actually putting a penny in the slot, since they had adapted the sets for use in pubs and clubs – 'We did very nicely with them,' he added. And to think that for years I had looked at this image of Miss Coomber as being no more than an elegant pose.

Commercial moving. The Mining Engineering Company Ltd was first established in Sheffield, but needs created by expansion led to its arrival in Worcester in 1925, which is probably when this photograph was taken. The wagon being unloaded is that of George Bury (Sheffield) Ltd.

On the opposite side of Bromyard Road, Eltex seem to have been around since the beginning of time. The GWR road transport about to carry off the latest load of wares has an air of antiquity about it.

To round off commercial matters, a few more pages of advertisements...

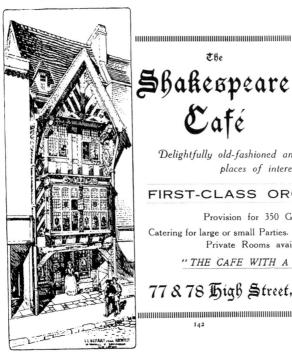

Modern Evening Wear

demands

**FINE
SNUG FITTING
LINGERIE**
to ensure perfect
line and appearance
of your ensemble.

●

HERE YOU WILL
FIND EVERYTHING OF
DAINTY CHARM
FOR THE MOST
EXACTING TASTES.

CENTRAL DRAPERY STORES
ST. SWITHIN STREET   -   -   WORCESTER

118

The "Bradman" Vase

Made specially by the Worcester Royal Porcelain Company to commemorate his unique achievement in scoring three successive double centuries on the Worcestershire County Cricket Ground.

This Vase, which is to be presented to Bradman on his return to Australia, may be seen during the next few days—together with plates autographed by the Australian Team—at the Porcelain Works Show Room.

The Worcester Royal Porcelain
COMPANY LIMITED.

The recipient of the 'Bradman' vase going out to bat at New Road on one of his three double century visits. Bradman first appeared there in 1930 (the year that Reg Perks joined the county) and scored 236. In 1934 he managed only 206, but made up for that in 1938 with 258. Perhaps it was the long interval before his final visit in 1948 that affected his play, for then he achieved but a single century.

W.W.D. had a framed print of this group in his office at Broad Street — it vanished, without trace, as did the original negative. Happily, Michael Vockins, the WCCC Secretary, very kindly — and spontaneously — unscrewed the pavilion copy from the wall and lent it to me for copying. From left to right: Perks, Howorth, Jackson and Martin, each of whom took over 100 wickets in the 1938 season.

A more sizeable group on the platform at the Public Hall. All I know about the event is that it was a 'Young Life Campaign' meeting. It is included by way of recording an administrative blot on the city's landscape, for the hall was demolished in June 1966, depriving the public of what had been its only proper concert/dance/exhibition/meeting hall. In its place there now stands – space, for cars and a weekend market.

My own photograph of the Public Hall, 3 May 1965.

At the beginning of the book I said that W.W.D. took his photography very seriously. It is therefore appropriate to conclude the selection with three of his serious photographs. The occasion in these two views was the unveiling of the County War Memorial at the cathedral on Armistice Day, 1922.

Finally, 'Woodbine Willie', who needs no further introduction. Of all the portrait sitters who came to W.W.D.'s studio, he was, without any doubt, the most respected. He came several times, despite self-disparaging opinions held on the subject of his features, which, I understand, he likened to those of 'a wizened monkey'. For me, this portrait has never been anything but that of a truly wise and great human being.

Few things in life work out according to plan, and this book is no exception to that exciting – if sometimes frustrating – rule.

Apart from the two photographs already seen, my contribution to *Worcester In Old Photographs* was intended to occupy no more than the last four pages of a 128 page book, but when delivery day dawned, I was greeted at the publishers' offices with glad tidings of a further 32 pages to be filled, a gesture of generosity reminiscent of Kensitas – I think it was Kensitas – who used to add an extra compartment to their cigarettes: 'And four for your friends'.

Since this particular 'extra compartment' consists entirely of my own photographs, its contents would be more accurately described as 'Worcester In Not So Old Photographs'. But 'old' is a peculiarly flexible term, especially in these times of rapid changes and transformations, so there may well be a few surprises to come for even the youngest reader.

Having stock-piled literally thousands of city photographs (enough to easily fill a couple of hundred books) selection has been far from easy. The final choice includes some notable events, regrettable disappearances, and well-known faces, whilst attempting to draw comparisons with a few of W.W.D.'s views. As with his major share of the pages, the photographs are arranged in neither logical nor chronological order, but are mostly linked by trains of rather silly thought, for which I apologise – though not too profusely.

THE CITY OF
WORCESTER
DATES BACK OVER 2000 YEARS.

• • •

CATHEDRAL
DATES FROM 1084.

• • •

GUILDHALL
DATES FROM 1721.

• • •

COMMANDERY
A PRE-REFORMATION HOSPITAL

• • •

THE WORCESTER
ROYAL PORCELAIN WORKS
EST. 1751.

• • •

ALL THE ABOVE ARE
OPEN TO VISITORS.

One of the old, city boundary signs that used to welcome and inform the arriving visitor. This one, photographed in March 1954, was in Spetchley Road, at a point roughly opposite the entrance to today's County Hall.

Two views from home. First, looking over snowy rooftops to the cathedral on 1 February 1956. The nearest roof formerly covered the premises of J.S. Wilcox the draper, but at this time an ice cream parlour, the Glacé Chalet, was in residence. Now, the Gas Board's highly individual blank wall stares across the street at the 'Bank wall' of the Midland. The lower view, taken in March of the same year and from the same vantage point, looks down Broad Street to the distant – now vanished – Electricity Works and All Saints church tower which is currently lacking its balustrade and pinnacles.

The first notable event of my photographic life was the visit of Winston Churchill, when he was made an Honorary Freeman of the City and joined a list of illustrious names that includes Lord Nelson, the Duke of Wellington, Sir Robert Peel, Earl Baldwyn and Sir Edward Elgar. He and Mrs Churchill received an enthusiastic welcome as they made their way up Broad Street, *en route* for the Guildhall. The year was 1950.

The crowd dispersing after its glimpse of 'Winnie'. The shop second from left was Johns & Son, specializing in tents, ropes and cord, besides supplying flags and bunting for special occasions like this.

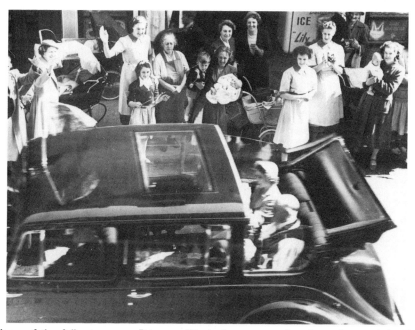

In June of the following year, Princess Elizabeth came to the city and toured the Royal Worcester Porcelain Works which was celebrating its bicentenary. As the royal car passed the Glacé Chalet, some of the watchers were too overcome to cheer and wave.

Not many waves here, either. Canoe on the canal at George Street in December 1956.

Canoodling on the quay. The Severn in flood at South Quay in September 1957.

The Worcester swans, whether at rest or in flight, were a familiar ingredient of the city. It was possible to get close to them at South Quay, where steps used to lead down to the water's edge. The steps have long since disappeared . . .

... but so have most of the swans. One of my saddest assignments was the photographing of RSPCA attempts to rescue and clean up oil-polluted birds in November 1965.

From swans' song to Armstrong's, whose Sansome Walk blind tells of their establishment in the reign of George III. Quite in keeping, then, for them to deliver costumes and suits by means of a four-wheeled box carriage, drawn by Broughton Supreme and seen here by the canal at Westbury Street in November 1965.

Same canal – different horse. The lock and old bridge at Sidbury, April 1957. The unharnessed motive-power being led to the lower level to continue its barge-hauling journey to Diglis. The old bridge was a narrow affair, dominated by the poster hoarding; its replacement, apart from being considerably wider, gives the passer-by a pleasing view of the lock and recently created canalside terrace by the Commandery.

The Swan Theatre opened on 27 June 1965 and was soon spreading its name around the city. The cat gave its own, more immediate performance.

Carrying publicity too far. Unfortunate neighbours in St Mary's Street, 1973.

Mobile publicity on a high-rise bicycle, propped against a pillar-box of society, whilst its stilted rider perambulates the Cornmarket in pursuit of business. 3 June 1954.

Cricket, in a roundabout way. The last appearance of a fair at New Road in June, 1967, with Pat Collins affording a framed picture of what used to be known as our National Game.

It was, once upon a time, traditional for cricketing tourists to play their opening match at Worcester, when they would also visit local factories by way of a little light relief. In Coronation Year it was the turn of the Australians, and here are two of my boyhood heroes, Keith Miller and Lindsay Hassett, engaged in conversation at Dent Allcroft's. It must have been on this occasion that a young apprentice approached me with a nervously-held autograph book: 'Excuse me, but are you Ian Craig?' 'No', I said, 'I'm local talent,' which was a shameful lie, for it was several more years before my latent abilities developed sufficiently to enable me to record my highest third class score of 13 against Cutnall Green, all in singles amassed in the astonishing time of 90 minutes.

When the West Indians came in 1950, Frank (later, Sir Frank) Worrell cast a critical eye over a pair of Dent's best. As one who averaged almost 50 in a career of 81 Test Match innings, he knew a bit about gloves.

Real glove and mitten weather. Flood, followed by February freeze, enabled skaters to polish their techniques on the County Ground in 1955.

Two questions: What is the connection between the two photographs? What is the significance of the scoreboard reading, 91 for 3? . . .

The answer to the first question: a boundary line. The farm was the County Ground's next door neighbour. This view gives the game away by revealing the electricity works in the background. But this was how it looked in February 1962. Today, both have gone; the farm has become a filling station; the electricity works was demolished several years ago. Worcester had a considerable number of farms within its boundaries. Those with longer memories might like to see how many they can remember. It would also be interesting to know if any city has ever had a farm as close to its centre as this.

The answer to the second question: it was the last score to appear on the old scoreboard at New Road. The occasion was, unfortunately, a minor match of limited appeal, so that few people were present for the tea interval unveiling and official opening of the new scoreboard on 4 May 1954. Note the air of thoughtful solemnity hovering over the proceedings.

There had been solemnity, too, when the city celebrated the Queen's Coronation on 6 June 1953 with a parade through the streets to Pitchcroft for a service of thanksgiving. Here, the Senior Service marches down Bridge Street.

The service at Pitchcroft. The Lord Lieutenant of Worcestershire, Admiral Sir William Tennant, salutes the standard of the British Legion.

Later, there was a fly-past by familiar, well-loved silhouettes, including 'Spitters', overhead.

Litter's underfoot, the day after. Loyalist left-overs in High Street, Sunday, 7 June 1953.

Just the man we've been looking for! A trifle late, but never mind. In April 1965, the county's first Litter Warden made his debut, in the person of Mr Stone.

Back to the Spitfire, just in time to say goodbye. For years, this one stood at the Perdiswell Headquarters of the Worcester 187 Squadron Air Training Corps. It was taken away on 7 February 1967.

In return, we've joined the 'Jet Set'.

It took a lot of jet power to control the fire at Lea & Perrins on the night of 24 August 1964. Despite the severity of the blaze, sauce production was held up for no more than ten days.

From running water to galloping Walker – if you'll pardon the apparent contradiction in terms.

Here he's slowed to a more reasonable pace, towards the end of a breathtaking display of canvassing on 14 March 1966.

Here's where the name-dropping really starts. In August 1952, *Tarzan's Savage Fury* was being screened at the Scala, with Tarzan and Jane making personal appearances for the benefit of their numerous admirers. I hardly knew where to put myself when, having photographed the general scene, I was invited to join them on an expedition. A chauffeur-driven Rolls pulled up at the cinema entrance and Tarzan, Jane and I got in to be driven to Gheluvelt Park for some gentle fish-spearing.

The fish-spearing, with privileged spectators.

More doubtfully privileged were the children forming a queue for the last Saturday morning 'Children's Club' at the Gaumont. The cinema closed later that day, 4 May 1974, with Peter Sellers in *Soft Beds, Hard Battles*, and an ironically-titled support film, *The Last Chapter*. The Scala had closed on 2 June 1973, with equal irony: *Bequest To The Nation*.

Ken Dodd's bequest to the nation is unlimited laughter. Off-stage he is — like many funny men — extremely serious. He came to Worcester on 31 May 1969, to open the Blackfriars Square Development...

...that made the old Angel Place unrecognizable. All these properties were demolished to make way for a covered market and new shops. Lewis Clarke's brewery tower is another local landmark to have disappeared.

The old Market Hall's High Street façade, all that was left of the building when photographed in June 1955. In recent years, Worcester has been playing a game of 'Musical Markets', the object of which is either to pull a market down and replace it with shops, or close a market and replace it with shops, having first moved the occupants of the covered market to an uncovered site. It's a whole lot of fun, provided you aren't one of the players.

Cripplegate House, at the far end of the park, November 1964. The house was demolished and was replaced in the late '60s by three blocks of flats.

The classic piece of city demolition: Marl Bank, Rainbow Hill, better known as Elgar's last home, from late 1929 until his death there on 23 February 1934. How much better it would have been to preserve it as an Elgar Museum, rather than – with no intended disrespect – the birthplace at Broadheath which knew him for no more than the first three years of his life. Sir Edward isn't forgotten by the city (though it once seemed that he had been) which has gone positively mad over 'Elgarizing' everything in sight, from the Duke of Wellington in Deansway to new houses on the site of the old Comer Gardens School – I'm sure Lord Nuffield wouldn't have minded – and, naturally, Marl Bank itself, so musically transformed into blocks of flats collectively known (when none of the letters are missing) as Elgar Court. Our heritage is safe. 25 April 1965.

As welcome relief from knocking-down, here is 'breaking-up', with an end of term collection of luggage in College Green. 1 April 1957.

More sadly, Witts' Closing-Down Sale at 48, High Street on 7 January 1966, and no shortage of ladies, milling about amongst the millinery.

Lovely boatering weather, higher up High Street, further on in time. A stormy afternoon in October 1971. The Midland Red double-decker obscures a few shop frontages . . .

. . . including the closed-down Josiah Stallard & Sons, wine merchants, established in 1642. Subsequent occupiers have retained the frontage, with Webster's currently proving that it is possible to put new books into an old wine merchant's without changing the label.

Russell & Bromley also kept faith with the past when adapting 27, High Street to the needs of the footsore. In August 1966 it was still Steward's, the long-established chemist and druggist, whose shop's interior may be seen, faithfully reconstructed, at the City Museum in Foregate Street.

Would that the same could be said of Beard's in Broad Street, whose original frontage and interior were equally pleasing to the eye. 23 November 1965.

High Street's comparatively recent conversion to a pedestrian precinct has already put these two scenes into the 'vintage' bracket. Both were taken at midday on Saturday, 3 August 1968.

The Shambles was taken over by pedestrians donkey's years ago. Only now – in June 1986 – is it being paved as such. The photograph shows it on its last day as a two-way street, in December 1963.

Mr and Mrs Page lived not far from the Shambles, but were enjoying a quiet Sunday morning sit-down at the Cross when I asked if I might photograph them. Their spontaneous, uncomplicated smiles made it a pleasure to do so. 30 July 1961.

Band in park. As part of the Salvation Army's centenary celebrations, its splendid band played for the first time in Cripplegate Park, conducted by Bandmaster Hooper. 9 May 1965.

Parking banned. It may seem strange that this book should almost reach its end on a note of restriction. It does so on the grounds that the subject matter is feminine and wearing hats. Worcester's first lady Traffic Wardens made their debut in May 1965, when Ann Jones and Enid Smith prepared to launch themselves on a public hitherto accustomed to mere male domination. Enid, intent on her note book, is happily doing the same job, 21 years later. As one who happens to like Traffic Wardens and has managed to avoid the ticket under the wiper, I offer two sound tips for penalty avoidance: 1. Never park in a 45 minute street and join the queue at the GPO. 2. Steer clear of the supermarket checkout if the customer in front shows any sign of paying by cheque.

This final page has been reserved for a piece of personal nostalgia. I spent many happy hours window-dressing at No. 8 and during our final months there in 1956, the emphasis was on W.W.D.'s earlier work, always guaranteed to attract attention. 6 February 1956.